ASHES

AND

SPARKS

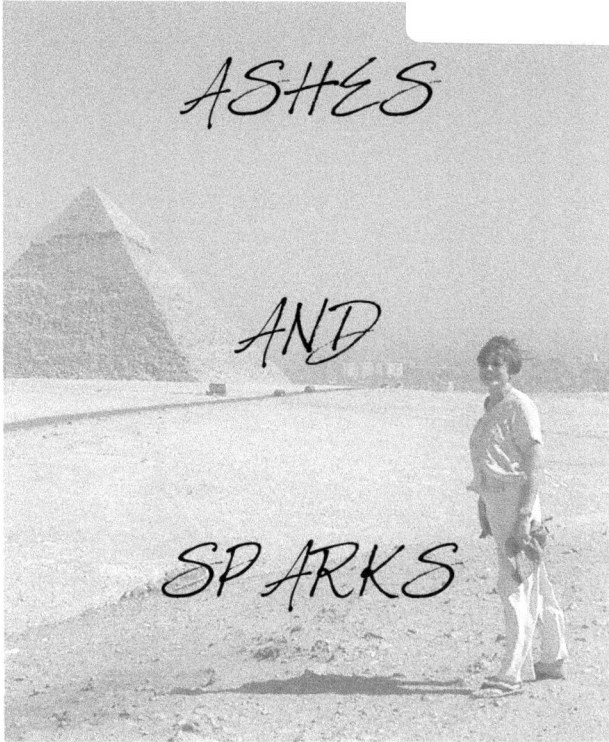

Sonia Waddell

Ashes and Sparks

978-1-935751-79-3

Scribbulations LLC

Many years ago, when I started writing occasional poems, I used to show them to my great friend and teacher, Tony Crisp (he who wrote *Yoga and Relaxation*, *Yoga and Childbirth*, *The Instant Dreambook*, etc.). One day he told me that he had sent one of my poems to a magazine and it had been published, and I remember being quite scared that my innermost feelings had been exposed for all to see. (That feeling soon passed, of course, and my next sensation was one of pride at having been published!)

However, a remnant of the original feeling persists today, and I admit to some nervousness at allowing these few poems (I have discarded many) into the light of day. It is just possible, though, that one or two may strike a chord with a reader, and that is my justification for, in the slightly adapted words of Percy Bysshe Shelley, "scattering, as from an unextinguished hearth, these Ashes and Sparks".

The final poem was inspired by a holiday in Egypt. Our group were given a camel-riding experience, and the owner of 'my' camel allowed me to go forward without him.

So my camel and I just went forward into the desert on our own, no one else around.

It was amazing.

Contents

ASHES

AND

SPARKS

The Rock

I stood on a rock,

With the salt spray swirling high,

And the wild wind rushing by,

And the sound of the waves as they beat on the rocks below.

And I heard the roar of the storm,

And I saw the great waves form,

And I felt that the deep was calling to me,

And I saw the Great Ones walking the sea,

And I knew that everything had to be,

And I said - I am here, below.

I dreamt this and wrote it down as soon as I awoke.

Sonia Waddell

Listen

Listen.

Listen to the voice of Nature,

As she rules her vast domain.

Eternal law, eternal symmetry,

Laughter and tears - and LOVE;

Gentle and tender, ruthless, strong,

And all-embracing.

Hear it, feel it, for a moment

Listen to the song.

Listen

In peace,

And hear a whisper of the Universe.

Deep, beauteous, vibrant, all-compelling,

Distant music,

Softly swelling,

Moving, reaching, calling,

Calling,

To the fastness of your soul.

Listen - and answer the call.

Sonia Waddell

Listening Within

My soul is full of music.
I cannot hear it,
But it sounds within me,
And sometimes a whisper rises to the surface
And fills me with intense pain and longing.
But I cannot express it.

I am too dull, too heavy and cumbersome.
I am unable to rise
Upon the wings of these far, distant, silver chimes,
Which play so sweetly and so poignantly
Within,
In the far corners of the Universe.

It does not matter.
I must content myself
With those few distant notes that now I hear.

And for the rest?
It comes into my thought
That I must live, and work, and be - myself, as now I am,
Before my ears may catch that fuller music,
Which now would rend me, shatter me, destroy me.

I am too small, too weak to listen to a longer note.

Victoria Station

Hurrying, jostling,
Nervously hastening,
Clutching their tickets and staring ahead.
Where are they going, those hundreds of passengers?
Are they the living, or are they the dead?

Do they realise the beauty
Within them, without them?
Do they notice the glory surrounding them all?
Are they listening - with happiness, joy, expectation,
Awaiting the moment of Life's urgent call?

How I long just to whisper,
One moment in passing,
You'll find it within you, still, quiet, and deep.
Pass beneath all the tumult, the sea's stormy surface;
Your spirit is waiting, to raise you from sleep.

All the beauty of life,
All the love that is in you,
Depths of knowledge and feeling, unknown before.
All are waiting and wondering,
Watching and pondering,
Listen - they call you - Oh, answer the call.

Sonia Waddell

The Wave

Formed in the measureless depths,
A ripple of foam, no more,
The wave goes forth on its journey,
Bound for the distant shore.

And anon it grows, increases,
In power, in force and might.
And it sweeps the endless ocean -
Though the shore's still out of sight.

It is sometimes rough and surly,
As it goes upon its way.
Then it wears a gleam of sunlight,
And is laughing, and kind and gay.

The winds may lash the surface
With their icy blasts, and shrill,
But within, in the cool depths,
It is ever peaceful and still.

And the restless fish are soothed,
And the weary ships caressed.
But the wave has come a long way,
And now it is seeking rest.

At last the land is sighted,
The wave need journey no more.
One last triumphant effort,
Then it sinks upon the shore.

The inspiration for this was a lovely painting I was given, of great waves crashing towards the shore.

Restlessness

I will seek restlessness,
And let it bear me where it will.
I will ride upon the dusty whirlwind
Of discontent -
And rest and sleep
And calm, delicious languor
Shall hold me not.

I will burst their bonds
And flee,
Ride forth into the desert
Of wild, arid imaginings,
Stride through the cool oasis
Of smug self-satisfaction,

And scale the searing rocks,
The jagged peaks
of discipline.

It is a long way still to go,
Towards the shining goal of everlasting peace.
But I will turn my face towards the goal,
And falter not, nor dally by the way.

I will seek restlessness,
And make it bear me where I will.

Sonia Waddell

This Was The Way

The sparrows singing in the tree,

I was the song they sung.

I was the rippling notes as they

Rose high above me to the sun,

And hovered

And fell back again

To whence they had begun.

I also was the clean, fresh air,

The drowsy stillness of the dawn,

The sparkling grass,

The whispering leaves,

The single feather on the breeze.

They were of me, and I of them;

And this was the way it had always been.

When I wrote this I was living in a small flat in South London. It had a tiny garden - with sparrows!

Prayer (1)

Dear God,

    Teach me to wish always

    That Thy will be done.

    To remember that everything that happens

    Is just a framework

    On which I can hang either good or ill results.

Sonia Waddell

Beauty

On a grey day
I looked into the clouds
Where they had parted,
And I saw a gentle radiance of golden, glowing colours,
Interspersed with rosy shadows.
Here was beauty.
And I felt uplifted
And inspired
And filled with all the radiance I had seen.
But then I looked around me, and about,
Where all had previously seemed dull and drear,
And there was beauty, too.
Growth, movement, life -
All stages of all being,
In changing hues and colours.
Some, indeed, were harsh and crude,
Unkind to look upon (when looked on as a single unit),
Others were nondescript;
And then, there were the many wondrous shades
Of shimmering fragility,
And glowing depth,
And strong and lustrous beauty.
And they all combined to make a great harmonious whole.

And this is beauty.
Where the rough, unlovely daubs of colour
(Which are but experiments with life)
Do meet the rainbow hues of universal spirit,
And combine, to blend into a great and perfect harmony.

Meditation

It is like a beautiful view
Just over the brow of a hill,
Or a sunset which you can barely see,
Though you press your nose against the window pane,
Or a raindrop, with a million, million reflections,
Or a dream, before you have woken.

Up and listen!
Harken!
Hark to the urgent call!
The pain in my breast it is ebbing,
And the moan of the wind is now far distant.
And the rustling of the great forests,
And the singing of the distant stars,
And the cry,
The cry of my inner Self,
It is fading,
Fading.

Sonia Waddell

The Storm Of Life

Laugh with the wind,

Live with the rain,

Love with the storm

As it blows you

And grows

In power and in glory,

Joyously plays with you,

Buffets your body.

Moves with immensity,

Majesty,

Mystery.

Brings with it beauty,

Joy, wonder, or misery.

Destroys you, creates you,

Makes you, and mars,

Laughs as you ponder,

Whence come these powers?

Stand in the silence

Inside the storm.

Safely it bears you

Quiet and warm.

Here is the true power,

Here the true light,

Past is the struggle,

Past is the fight.

These awesome mysteries,

Whence do they come?

You know as well as I

Since we are one.

Pass through the outer shell,

Seek the true man.

Look for the Inner Self,

ATMAN, I AM.

This is one of my favourite poems. Storms do bring wild and wonderful thoughts and inspirations.

Tears

So many tears.

What good are they?

The ache is always there,

And the sharp pain comes stabbingly.

Oh, God, where am I, who am I,

Why, please why?

Still the tears flow.

Oh God, please explain.

The All-Present Waters

I come from the sea,
And thereto will I return.
I am of its very essence,
And I feel it, deep within me,
And around,
Stretching all places,
Filling every void.
There is no empty hole
Or gaping cavity,
The sea fills all.

Have you felt it?
Do you hear
The roaring violence in your ears,
The leap of gentle ripples,
Rising,
Falling,
Deeply surging
With the tide?

Oh, mighty water!
Let me come
Into your being.
Let me rise and fall within you,
Moving to your every rhythm.
Let me throw myself entirely
Into the deep waters.

Sonia Waddell

The Grave

Old man ,
Storm-shaken,
Bent and gnarled,
With stricken arms aloft
He shows his grief
In wild lament
Before the ravaged grave.
Over the trampled earth he bows his head
In wondering sorrow,
Alone.

Up, and away!
Why should you weep?
Why show distress?
This sinful act -
It happens all the time,
It happens every day,
And we are not distressed,
We turn the other way.
We care not -
It is best
This way.

Get up and go,
In carefree ignorance.
Leave your woe
To fester in this desecration.
It is better so.

And still he kneels, lamenting.

Now they come to take him, chained, away.
He had no right to care,
To grieve, to interfere.
He must be taught to stand aloof,
And let the world go its own way
To self-destruction.

*Sometimes I become overwhelmed by all the sadness, misery and "uncaringness" around me.
But there is, of course, so much kindness and beauty and the will to do good.*

Sonia Waddell

The House

I am like a house
With a number of doors and windows
And little sky-lights.
And some of these are open,
But a great many are still tightly closed.

Or I am like one of those cardboard toys
Which a child has,
With a lot of little fastened shutters.
And he hangs the toy above his bed,
And each night, during the month before Christmas,
He opens another shutter,
And finds another exciting picture,
Until, on Christmas Eve,
He has opened them all,
And he knows all the secrets of his toy.

But my Christmas Eve is a long way away,
And there are some shutters
Which I cannot open
Just yet,
Because I would only find within
A mass of bewildering information
Which would mean nothing to me.
I shall open them when I am older.

For others I have the key in my hand,
And I will open them one day
When I hear the voice I am waiting for,
Speaking the words I can understand.
Then I shall open them wide, and let the warm sunshine in.

Sonia Waddell

Primrose

This primrose -
I picked it from the gentle, dewy bank where it had root.
I pulled it from the damp brown earth,
Moss-covered,
Fragrant with dead leaves,
Young buds,
And hidden sunshine.

Then
It was a part of all it fed upon,
And of the new growth,
Quickened in decay,
And of the soil,
The shrubs,
The trees,
The earth, the air,
And of all moving creatures -
They were one.

Now I have picked it!
Is it dead?
Does it still live?
(Or had it ever life?)
Yes, for it breathed
And poured forth fragile scent,
And gave itself as beauty to the world.
It was -
And thus it lived.

And still it is,
And shames me with its generous giving.

And even as I pulled it from the ground,
And took it in my hands,
And looked upon it -
In that instant
I became this primrose.
In a silent moment
I was part
Of all the mighty process of becoming.
I became
What I had ravaged.

Sonia Waddell

To My Husband

The trees, the stones, the sea,

The earth, the air,

The shadow and the substance,

All are but

Manifestations of my love for you.

They are my love.

Together we are one

In loving.

Pouring forth

All beauty, life, and being.

Great and mighty,

Small and fragile,

All pervading and all knowing,

Like the oceans, deep and peaceful,

And the heavens, in their splendour,

Or the dewdrop, in its wonder ....

All the world is life and loving.

All the world is of my loving.

Prayer (2)

Oh, God,

Here is my prayer.

There is so much I long to do.

I want to make beautiful things,

To express myself in painting, music, words, speech.

To help others,

To love truly.

I am so small and ineffectual,

And, in spite of the ache of unfulfillment

Within me,

I achieve nothing.

Please God,

Help me at least to love, and make other people happy,

And to do your will.

Amen.

On The Bus

I sat beside her on the bus.
Later she turned and spoke to me,
Nothing of importance, just a friendly word.
And I replied,
And we conversed throughout the journey.
She was 79 and in love with life,
And her life she said had been hard,
But I saw the glint in her eye
And I basked in her merry smile.

I waved farewell when I left the bus,
And I doubt I will see her again.
But we each gave love to the other,
And that will go on for ever.

Sonia Waddell

The Bud

This was a bud,
And here the parent stem,
Which first had formed within the rich, dark earth
(A seed, a fragile shoot),
And then had grown
Upwards
Seeking the light,
While down into the depths had gone the roots.

For long the bud was tightly closed,
Perhaps afraid of wind and rain?
Ashamed to show, to look upon, its core?
Had it forgotten how to open?

It curled within itself,
And longed to open to the gentle air,
But knew not where to start,
And was afraid of pitiless exposure.

Still the winds caressed it,
And the rains bathed it
Gently,
And sometimes a great storm blew,
Wild and unleashed,
And revelled in its glory,
And the sun smiled on it.

And then one day the bud felt soft stirrings within,
A lightness all around.
Gone was the weight of fear.

The outer husk did crack and fall away,
And the soft petals
Opened
One by one,
Gently,
Gradually,
Until all lay revealed.

It leant upon the wind,
It bathed in warmth and light,
It loved,
And it knew peace.

Sonia Waddell

Sea Dream

Remember how once you gambolled
And roamed in the blue-green sea?
And dived to the depths
With a powerful twist
Of your supple self,
Or, arrow-like,
Sped like a dream to a distant shore,
To explore
The jewelled coast of a fabled isle?

You knew to the full
The happiness
Of giving yourself to the sea;
Of surrendering entirely
To the movement of the sea;
Of the great, supporting waters,
As you lay in the breast of the sea.
And you basked in the sun,
And rolled in the waves,
And let them bear you free,
And gave yourself completely
To the cradle of the sea.

And now I am coming with you
Into the arms of the sea.
Together we'll dance in the shallows,
Together we will be free
Of the ocean's furthest boundaries,
Of its secrets hidden and deep.
And I'll teach you again to give yourself,
As you would to the arms of sleep,
Into the heart of the all-embracing,
All-pervading Deep.

Another dream. The sea, and thoughts of the sea, and dreams of the sea,
have always played a big part in my life.

Sonia Waddell

After Loss

I will walk with you

Through each successive dream

That life unfolds.

And if one dreaming self

Should lose the other -

Among the changing shadows -

Yet will our souls stand joyfully together,

Watching and waiting, listening sometimes

To the music of the changeless, the eternal.

Moving forward through the dreams together.

I wrote this after the sudden death of our daughter.

Autumnal Rhythm

Swooping down the wind,
Curving and gliding with abandoned grace,
The autumn leaves are dancing in the sky.
What is this random chase?
The sky is dark with moving forms,
Dead leaves,
All shapes and many-coloured,
Rising and falling in the dance.
Moving by chance,
Or in obedience to indifferent law?

A single leaf whirls by,
Without direction.
Impotent in choice
It flutters to its rest.
Another swoops before

There is an ordered rhythm
In this chaotic fluttering.
Though rebel leaf should soar above the troop,
Drifting on high,
Or transient fellows wander to the ground,
A motley heap,
Scattered awry,
Stand back and see
They each are part
Of one great harmony.

Sonia Waddell

Mist

A rushing multitude of thoughts

Seeking expression,

Eyes bright with tears.

It is the intense beauty of the day

- The world - The people -

Singing to me, out of the greyness.

I hear the music of the voices,

And the deep splendour of the poetry

Of many hearts,

Singing, singing:

When will you learn to be, only to be?

To stand amidst the surging waves of beauty,

And let the music soak your every fibre?

To learn to move

Softly and gently,

  ·acefully,

    ·ful unison

      ` great orchestra of Being?

        ·iness!

          ·ic fades

You Are Always Asking Me

You are always asking me
What I believe,
And when I tell you
You are displeased.
You ask me to explain
The very core of my being,
And you are irritated when I falter,
Unable to tell
Of spacious endings and beginnings;
Of the light which my eyes
Are yet learning to see,
In speech you would understand.

How can I tell you
Of the grandeur of the idea,
Of unity
And the truth that is in all things?
Your mind says, That is a lie,
You have no proof.
And my heart says, I KNOW.

Sonia Waddell

Who Am I?

Who am I?
The call re-echoed through myself,
Still, calm and deep,
And present everywhere.
It roused me from my sleep.
I listened to the cry,
And wondered, Who am I?
And sought the answer through the mists of memory.

And as the time passed by
I heard myself reply.
I answered, I am nothing.

Nothing? or everything?
I knew them as the same,
And I was filled with peace and calm content.

Lethargy

The sun moves slowly down towards the horizon,
And the air is soft and fragrant
And misty,
With unusual shades of pink and blue and violet,
And vague, indeterminate colours.

It seems quite solid.
Movement has slowed down,
And people drift between the motes of dust
And shades of light,
With heavy bodies,
Laggard footsteps.

They are puzzled.
Why are they so slow?
And what should they be doing, and where going?
Their minds are fumbling, groping in the fog.

Where is the purpose that they knew,
The place of consciousness and great decision
(Not drugged uncertainty)?
Where is the lightness, and the gentle grace,
The insubstantial form, and fleeting pace?

A distant memory emerges from the twilight,
And a star shines in the distance.

Sonia Waddell

A Brief Realisation

How strange!
I have given up my identity.
I am now a part of life
And all that is.
I am beginning to fit into that great
And everlasting
Pattern of the universe.

It seems
That I need never make another difficult decision.
By merely listening inwardly
They will be made for me.

It is a lovely feeling
Of belonging.

Of course, that lovely feeling never lasts for long.

Paradox

Forward!

Not backward-looking whence we came,

But onward striving t'wards the same.

Our goal is ever sure.

Since time is meaningless

We know that we

Will one day reach that vast Eternity

Wherein we now abide.

A paradox indeed!

Silence

Silence.
Its moments are so beautiful,
Full of a multitude of sounds and voices,
Coming from the same source,
Bringing the same message.
They fade into the distance
And dissolve,
Fragile
And elusive in their quality.

The voices of this silence
Are but one voice,
Which sounds deep upon the inner ear
Of peaceful receptivity.

I hear them coming,
Gently, slowly, imperceptibly,
"Be still, and know that I am God".
I listen - but I do not listen.
And I hear - but do not hear.
And I am caught up,
And become
Part of the silence
And the many voices.

And they are
Through me, with me, of me,
Are myself.
They are the silent, motionless becoming;
The moving, urgent music of the spheres;
The present sound of all creation.

Sometimes I hear and am this silence,
In the midst of all the busy living of the world
And its affairs.
The silence is within,
And the outer is but a help,
Never a hindrance.

But many times
My ears are full of all my wild imaginings,
And I can hear nothing
But emptiness.
And having known the silence
I feel its loss
Acutely.

Sonia Waddell

Egyptian Reverie

I sit among the reeds by the river bank
And rest,
And watch the slow clouds move across the sky,
And the gentle ripples shiver on the silver surface before me.
I am weary.
It is a long journey I am on,
But it is always pleasant to rest by the beautiful flowing
Waters of an oasis.

Soon I will return to my wanderings in the desert.
My beautiful desert, how I love you!
The hot sun awaits me,
And the dry wind blows before me,
And the unending sands stretch forever.
My spirit lifts at the prospect
And I open my arms wide to embrace it all.

And now the ibis stands in the shallows, seeking his frog,
And a silver fish leaps nearby.
A lion roars in the distance.

Will He come, steering his boat, He for whom I am waiting?
He will come when the time is right.

Maybe I will wander and return many times
Before I see Him.

About The Author

Sonia Waddell is a physiotherapist and an animal activist. After retiring from hospital work, she became a school speaker on vegetarianism, and she also campaigns against the cruelty involved in vivisection, factory farming, live animal export, and hunting.

9 781935 751793